BUT WHAT DO I DO WITH MY FEET?

A Pianist's Guide
to the Organ

Janette Fishell

Abingdon Press
Nashville

To all my students,
former, current, and future,
and
to my mentor in the field of church music,
Wilma Jensen,
who first taught me the wisdom of the phrase
Laborare est orare
"To labor is to pray"

BUT WHAT DO I DO WITH MY FEET?
A Pianist's Guide to the Organ

Copyright © 1996 by Abingdon Press

This book is printed on recycled, acid-free paper.

ISBN 0-687-01036-5

99 00 01 02 03 04 05—10 9 8 7 6 5 4 3 2

MANUFACTURED IN THE UNITED STATES OF AMERICA

Contents

Prelude

Taking a new step, uttering a new word, is what people fear most.
Dostoyevsky

Increasingly pianists are taking that first step toward being "Sunday morning organists" with little or no formal organ training to assist them on their journey. Whether you are eager to play the organ or are a "reluctant organist" who has been literally pressed into service, the material contained in this book will help you meet, without fear, the technical and musical challenges that await.

I would like to thank the following persons who offered me support and critical insights during the writing of this book: Patrick Hawkins, Wilma Jensen, Nathan Williams, Malcolm Tait, and Shirley Kuhn who also prepared my manuscript for publication. Special thanks go to my husband, Colin Andrews, whose love, patient support, and musical insights sustained me throughout this project.

Janette Fishell
Associate Professor
School of Music
East Carolina University
Greenville, N.C.

Chapter One
Bourdons, Boxes, and Benches—A Brief Guide to the Organ

In my work with new organists I have found that the organ, with its multiple keyboard and mysteriously numbered stops, can be very frightening to those accustomed to the piano's eighty-eight keys. I will not forget the student who, touching the organ keys for the first time, seemed relieved that she didn't receive an electric shock! The information below is only the briefest of guides into this "unknown region." Let it begin your journey toward a more confident understanding of the limitless possibilities of the "King of Instruments."

A. Keyboards

The organ's keyboards, called **manuals**, have the following standardized names, listed in typical order from top to bottom:

English/U.S.	French	German
Swell	Récit	Oberwerk, Brustwerk, or Schwellwerk
Great	Grand Orgue*	Hauptwerk
Choir (or Positive)	Positiv*	Positif (or Rückpositif)

* May be in reverse order

The Great is considered the main manual division with other manuals acting as secondary divisions. The Pedal division completes the organ's specifications and when providing the bass line should be used to balance the manuals in terms of dynamic and timbre. The Swell is located in a box behind **shades,** which are opened and closed with the **expression pedal** (sometimes referred to as the **swell pedal**). Organs may have other so-called expressive divisions that can be made to sound louder or softer by means of expression pedals (most commonly the Choir division), or may not have any enclosed divisions. This is particularly true of organs designed with Baroque models in mind.

B. Stops

The organ's pipes (organized in sets called **ranks**) are controlled by stops or tabs that are marked with the name of the characteristic color of the rank. In addition, a number and footage sign (e.g., 8') or a Roman numeral are also notated. This is usually the first source of serious anxiety for the Sunday morning organist since such labels are foreign to the piano. To combat this stop "angst," read the following and then test your new-found knowledge at several different organs.

1. Families of Stops

Despite the plethora of stop names, there are actually only four main groups of tonal families.

a. **Principals** are the foundation of the organ. This is the true "organ tone," which is not imitative of any other instrumental color and is the backbone of hymn registrations and organ repertoire. (Other names: Montre, Diapason, Prestant, Octave)

b. **Flutes,** as their name implies, are imitative of the orchestral instrument. There is much variety in flute tone, from very powerful solo harmonic flutes to soft Gedackts and Bourdons. (Common flute types: Bourdon, Subbass, Gedackt, Stopped Diapason, Rohrflöte, Nachthorn)

c. **Strings,** like flutes, are imitative stops that display a wide variation in color. (Common string types: Salicional, Gamba, Viole de gamba)

A note on **Célestes:** Both flute and string ranks may include stops marked céleste. These stops are tuned either sharp or flat and, when used with their "partner" ranks that are "straight" (tuned to regular A440 pitch), they produce a shimmering, undulating tremolo effect. Céleste ranks should always be used with the straight rank, but the straight rank with regular tuning may be used alone or in combination with other ranks. For example, the string rank Salicional 8' is "straight" and may be used alone or with its partner céleste rank, the Voix Céleste. The Voix Céleste may not be used alone and should always be used with the Salicional. Do not use céleste ranks in the full ensemble that combines the larger resources of the organ.

d. **Reeds** encompass sounds that are imitative of the orchestral reed family (oboe, clarinet, bassoon) and brass family (trumpet, trombone, tuba). Because of positioning and power some reeds are solo ranks, such as the Trompette en Chamade. (Common reed ranks: Hautbois, Cromorne, Posaune, Cremona, Schalmei)

2. Pitches

a. Numbers designating pipe length/pitch

Even those with the worst case of math anxiety can easily understand the meaning of the Arabic numbers found on stops. Play middle C on the Principal 8' stop, a pitch that corresponds to middle C on the piano. The stop is labeled 8' because the lowest pipe is approximately eight feet long. Now play the same key but with a stop marked 4' and you will notice that the pitch is one octave above middle C. In like manner, the 16' is one octave below and the 2' is two octaves above. All stops on the organ whose Arabic numbers are divisible by 1 (i.e., 32', 16', 8', 4', 2', 1') are part of the unison/octave ranks and form the body of the organ's **ensemble** or chorus.

Fractions, called **mutations** or overtone stops, most often come in two forms: the ranks sounding a *fifth* above the 8' fundamental and those sounding a *third* above the fundamental. When one pulls a stop marked 2 ⅔' and plays middle C, the actual *pitch* played is one octave and a fifth above middle C. Repeat the exercise with a stop marked 1 ⅗' and the pitch played is two octaves and a third above middle C. In the next chapter, we will see how these mutations can be used to great effect when combined with fundamental stops.

b. Roman numerals

Stops with Roman numerals indicate **compound stops** that control more than one set of pipes.

Mixtures are the most common compound stops. They most often have unison, octave and fifth-sounding (2 ⅔' series) ranks. The Roman numeral designates the number of ranks sounding and, in the case of some mixtures, the number of ranks may change in successive octaves (e.g., Mixture VI-VIII designates a mixture that adds ranks as it ascends). Mixtures are never used alone but are combined with the 8' foundation (Principal) and other ranks as needed to build a brilliant chorus that is often designated **Organo Pleno** or **Plenum**.

Mutation complexes combine the "fraction" stops described above on one stop. The **Sesquialtera** is the most common and contains, on one stop, both the 2 ⅔' (twelfth above the fundamental) and the 1 ⅗' (seventeenth above the fundamental). Use this with Flute 8' (and perhaps Flutes 4' and/or 2') as a solo, especially in Baroque music.

C. The Well-accessorized Organ

1. Pistons and Couplers

a. **Pistons** are numbered buttons found above or below manuals and/or over the pedal board that change stop combinations. Pistons that affect the entire organ are called **General** pistons and those changing individual manuals or pedal only are **divisional** pistons. They are set by depressing a **setter piston,** by holding the piston in while setting stops, or by setting switches located on a **setter board**. Many organs contain **reversible** pistons that control **couplers** (see below), thereby facilitating quick reductions and additions of stops.

b. **Couplers** are devices that unite one division with another and may couple at unison (8'), suboctave (16') or super-octave (4') pitch levels. For example, the Swell to Great 8' brings the stops pulled on the Swell to the Great at normal pitch level; the Swell to Great 4' brings those stops to the Great one octave higher. Some organs have **intra-manual couplers** that double the sound of the manual's own drawn stops either at the suboctave (Great to Great 16') or super-octave (Great to Great 4').

c. **Coupler memory** is found in various forms—from a few levels controlled by manual dial to hundreds of levels of memory with digital read-out. Most systems feature clearly marked setter buttons and can be locked for security.

2. Other Accessories

The **tremulant** is the organ's "vibrato" stop, which should be used with great discretion and never with the full ensemble. The **unison off** cancels the sound from a given division at normal pitch and is useful when one wishes to couple to a manual but not use the stops drawn for that division. The **crescendo pedal** is programmed (either by the organ maker or by the organist using the computer memory) to gradually add all chorus stops until **full organ** is achieved. Most organists experience, at least once, the unpleasantness of confusing the crescendo pedal with the swell pedal—invariably during the quietest moment of Communion!

D. Approaching the Bench

Unfortunately most organs in this country do not automatically come with adjustable benches. While raising bench height is easily accomplished through the addition of wooden blocks, many benches are *too high* to begin with. Organists who are short, or those whose legs are disproportionately short, can develop serious shoulder and back problems if they play for an extended period on a bench that is too high. Playing on a bench that is too high is rather like asking a pianist to perform while seated on the floor. If your instrument doesn't have an adjustable bench, explain the benefits of one to the appropriate people in your church. If this doesn't work, ask permission to have the legs cut to a desired height, explaining that well-made but inexpensive wooden blocks of various heights will provide all the variation needed for other organists using the instrument. You may even have a woodworker in your congregation who can make a simple bench.

While there is no formula for determining bench height, follow these steps to determine what "feels" right. Experimenting with bench height requires that you find an adjustable bench or a bench that is low enough to give you an adequate "base" height from which to start. Check with other church organists or local music schools in your community until you find an organ bench that can help you find your ideal, then use a tape measure to mark your optimum height.

Sit "centered" on the bench with your left foot over C and your right over E. Your "rockers" or "sit bones" should be placed well toward the back of the bench, not in the middle, so that at least half of the length of the thighs is comfortably resting on the bench (see diagram 1). Now allow the feet to rest on keys C and E and depress. If you cannot do this without straining forward, the bench is too high. If you strain to keep your feet from playing when you do not wish them to, the bench is too low.

Good "centering" on bench: Torso is balanced on "sit bones" and a full range of relaxed motion is possible.

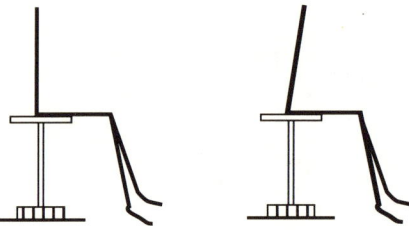

Bad body position: Torso leans or curves back excessively; tension reduces range of motion and causes physical pain and technical insecurity.

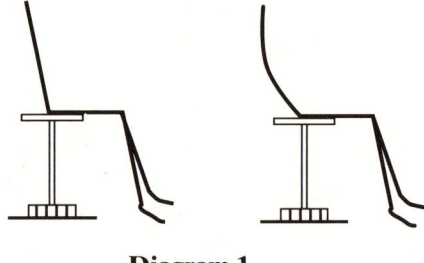

Diagram 1

Chapter Two
An Introduction to the Art of Registration

Every science begins as philosophy and ends as art.
Will Durant

Registration is most certainly an art, no matter how mathematical the organ might appear at first sight. What is needed is a certain amount of historical and practical knowledge combined with an inquisitive mind and a keen ear. The great organists J. S. Bach and César Franck were known for the power and beauty of their registrations, yet it was said by their contemporaries that both men registered in ways considered novel for their time. While there are some general "truths" in registration, all organists recognize that each instrument is individual. Prescribed stop combinations are helpful in developing a sound "ideal" for a particular piece, but one must almost always experiment to achieve the best effect on each instrument.

A. Graded Pistons

The first lesson in registration for service playing that my students learn is to **grade** all divisional and general pistons. Starting with the softest sounds, set each piston progressively louder until the full ensemble is achieved. This allows you to effect a smooth crescendo or decrescendo by "playing the pistons" (i.e., moving up or down the pistons). It also means that you are never far from salvation if the wrong stop or piston is added since the organ is "set up" in a logical fashion.

Although exact prescriptions are impossible to devise due to the vast amount of variation in organ specifications, the following scheme for grading divisional pistons may be used as a guideline. For organs with fewer pistons, combine these steps; conversely, for those with more than five divisional pistons, increase the number of gradations, thereby gaining subtlety to the overall crescendo. Finally, these pistons may be used to produce graded general pistons or, in the absence of any divisional pistons whatsoever, one may use these combinations as general gradations. Those playing organs with computer memories should have one memory setting that is entirely graded. In the past I have had "first service" graded pistons that were softer than the "second service" pistons for the benefit of those early churchgoers who were not quite prepared for the full glories of the organ at 8:00 A.M.

B. Hymns and Repertoire

Unfortunately anything more than the most basic overview of registration for the service is beyond the scope of this book. All "reluctant organists" are advised to consult one of the recommended resources listed in Appendix III for more detailed explanations and guidelines. It is hoped that the information below will help new organists take the first steps toward more confident registration in hymns and service music.

1. Hymns

Variation in hymn registration should stem from the text and general character of the hymn tune. While one should strive for musical interest through well-considered registration changes, too frequent or overly fussy changes can detract from the dignity of the hymn and deflect attention away from the hymn's text to the organist's skill.

a. **Basic hymn registration** should begin with the Great Principal chorus consisting of Principals 8', 4', and 2'. Draw the Pedal Principal 16', 8', and 4' and the Great/Pedal coupler. Listen for good balance between divisions and adjust as needed.

b. **Secondary divisions** (Swell, Choir, or Positive) may be coupled to the Great (and Pedal). Begin with an 8' foundation (Principal or Flute) and "build" the manual chorus by adding Flute or Principal 4' and 2'. Do not include célestes or tremulants in the chorus.

Example of Graded Divisional Pistons

Piston #	Swell	Choir/Positive	Great	Pedal*
1	Salicional 8' + Voix Céleste or Flute 8' + tremolo	Flute 8' + Swell/Choir 8'	Flute 8' + Choir/Great 8+ and Swell/Great 8'	soft Flutes 16' and 8' + Swell/Pedal 8'
2	foundations 8' minus céleste	foundations 8'	foundations 8'	same
3	same + foundations 4' and possibly a small reed 8'	same + foundations 4'	same + foundations 4'	foundations 16' and 8'
4	same + foundations 2' and mixture (possibly minus reed 8')	same + foundations 2'	same + foundations 2' and mixture	same + Octave 4' and reed 8' or 16'
5	same + all reeds and remaining mixtures	same + reed 8'	same + reed 8'	same + remaining reed

* Throughout the grading process, care should be taken to maintain good pedal/manual balance. While it is preferable to retain pedal independence by avoiding the Great/Pedal coupler, this is sometimes impossible. Try adding Swell and Choir to Pedal first, only adding Great to Pedal if the Pedal is completely lacking in support.

    c. **Reeds** may be added to the manual and pedal choruses for a richer sound. Do not add very large, piercing solo reeds such as the Trompette en Chamade to the chorus.

    d. **Mixtures** may be added to the manual choruses for a more brilliant sound.

    e. **Softer congregational hymns** may be successful on all of the 8' foundations (perhaps even including the célestes on rare occasions). I use this rarely, but with great effect, on softer, expressive hymns my congregation knows extremely well (e.g., "Silent Night" on Christmas Eve). Use this soft hymn registration only when the congregation doesn't need the organ for leadership but merely to "fill out" the harmony and provide a nice "aura" around the singing. If you are fortunate enough to play for a church that can sing well-known hymns *a cappella,* use a softer registration to prepare them for the organ's "dropping out" on one stanza.

f. **Playing hymn melodies** in the right hand with left hand and pedal accompaniment is an excellent method of registrational variation, and can even double as a hymn voluntary or prelude! Right hand solo combinations:

Reed 8' (support with 8', 4' as needed)

or: *Flutes 8', 4', 2', 2 ⅔', 2', 1 ⅗'

or: *Flutes 8', 4', 2', plus Sesquialtera II

(*This combination, called a **Cornet,** is very useful as a solo color in much organ repertoire, especially Baroque.)

2. Repertoire

Much organ repertoire contains registration suggestions provided by composers or editors. It is safe to assume that music published in this century contains, for the most part, authoritative registration indications that reflect the wishes of the composer. This is often not the case in older, historic music, which might include inappropriate and unauthentic registrations, articulations, and phrasing added by an editor. Repertoire lists in Appendix II will provide suggested editions. When in doubt about which edition to buy, consult a local authority, a music dealer who specializes in organ music, or one of the sources listed in Appendix III. Some general guidelines for stylistic registration follow.

Baroque music should be registered for clarity. Avoid "duplicating" ranks (i.e., using both Principal 8' and Flute 8') when one will suffice. Solo melodies sound most stylistic using a mutation complex (see Sesquialtera or Cornet above) or a reed stop such as the Trumpet or Cromorne with or without a 4' foundation to aid speech and carrying power. The tremulant was known in the Baroque so feel free to use it for solos, but do not use the céleste. One beautiful but neglected choice is using the Flute 4' (or even Principal 4') alone. This provides a nice respite from 8' tone and is especially charming in English voluntaries. Of course, the use of the Principal 8' or Flute 8' alone is the essence of simplicity and, on well-voiced organs, beauty.

Nineteenth-century or **Romantic** repertoire should be registered for a more homogeneous sound. Homophonic (chordal) textures are apt vehicles for the warm, rich foundations (8' Principals, Flutes, and Strings) and may include small reeds such as the Oboe 8'. The céleste, always with its partner straight rank, is appropriate here, but avoid using it for every prelude if you want to prevent its becoming a "Sunday morning cliché." A beautiful, warm solo/accompaniment for music in this style consists of:

Solo on Great with 8' foundations + Swell/Great
Accompaniment on Swell 8' Flutes, Strings and Célestes

Try this with the solo down one octave in the tenor range, especially if your Principal is very strong or bright.

Twentieth century **Contemporary** compositions are more uniformly explicit in their registrations so general guidelines are unnecessary. As in all the styles mentioned above, the overriding principles of registration may be summed up by the "three B's": Balance, Blending, and Beauty.

C. Electronic Organs

Electronic organs have benefited greatly from recent technological advances. Those playing one of the more recently built electronic organs may be able to use the ideas in this book with little or no alteration. For others, some additional advice is necessary.

The Hammond

Many of this country's most celebrated organists have encountered a Hammond at least once in their careers and many, I venture to guess, had no idea what to make of those drawbars and black keys on first sight. Any organist who plays a Hammond on a regular basis should find a copy of Steven Irwin's *Dictionary of Hammond Organ Stops* (G. Schirmer, 1939), which provides a thorough overview of this type of organ's disposition. In the meantime, the information following will provide some basic concepts of registration for both large and spinet Hammonds.

Hammond organ registrations are determined by two means: through the two rows of black pre-set keys (set at the factory) and through the harmonic drawbars (two sets of nine drawbars for each of the two manuals and two drawbars for the pedal). There are other features such as **vibrato** (tremulant), **chorus** (céleste for the entire organ), and **echo** (artificial reverberation). As with pipe organ registration, the vibrato and chorus should be used sparingly and never combined in service playing with larger, more powerful principal chorus registrations.

At first it is perhaps safest to rely on the pre-set keys, which provide a range of solo colors and chorus registrations. For those wishing more variety, the world of the harmonic drawbars must be entered. While the result is far from the sound of an actual pipe organ, the drawbars do allow the player to actually "voice" the organ stop by determining the overtone of each registration. A Clarinet 8' is set 00 4160 431, while a Flute 8' is 00 8870 000, the numbers reflecting the difference in the makeup of the overtones of each stop. By following the number "recipes" provided in music and in Irwin's book, an organist can create a myriad of colors.

Larger Hammond organs have pedalboards with smaller ranges and different dimensions than modern American pipe organs. However, traditional legato heel/toe technique can be used (see chapter 4). It is the spinet model's one octave pedalboard that is undeniably the greatest challenge to the service player. Its restricted range and rather awkward dimensions have contributed to the development of the infamous "left-footed" organist. While traditional pedal technique is useless here, there are some musical solutions to the problems posed by the spinet.

a. **Shoes:** Rather than playing in stockings, try ballet slippers or "character" shoes available from a dance supply store. These should allow you to feel the rather awkward pedals while you avoid going shoeless in church, which can, after all, seem a bit undignified.

b. **Hymns:** Circle chord roots and play only these notes, adding pedal points whenever possible. Play by alternating left and right feet on successive pedals (for clarity) for legato line as much as you can.

c. **Legato music** for manuals often sounds best on electronic organs, given the immediate sound decay that is characteristic of most electronic organs. This repertoire conveys a more pleasant "singing line" than does music in a more vertical, detached style. Manuals-alone music is a staple of all new organists' service music and so it travels well to all sorts of organs.

Chapter Three
Making Music on the Manuals

It is obvious that reluctant Sunday morning organists who are making the transition from piano to organ need to become acclimated to manual touch and to technique long before the pedals are used to any great extent. The following sections address fundamental touch concepts, crucial fingering guidelines, a practical approach to manuals-alone hymn playing and suggestions for repertoire.

A. Developing Touch at the Organ

As in piano technique, there are two general categories of touch: legato and non-legato (the latter is often called detached or **"détaché"**). Both contain many degrees of variation, from over-legato to brightly detached staccato, and it is the aim of all musicians to achieve many subtle gradations within this broad spectrum of possibilities.

This common ground notwithstanding, there are two important differences between the piano and organ that influence one's approach to touch (i.e., key attack and release). The first is that pipes cease to speak immediately upon a key's release; the organ's only sustaining capability is provided by a room's acoustic. The second and less obvious difference is that the pipe organ is a wind instrument played by keys, whereas the piano is a percussion instrument with keyboard. The first condition requires careful control over the length of notes; the second calls for a sensitivity to the method of depressing and releasing the key.

1. Legato

While it is an over-simplification to say, as I have often heard, that "organ touch is legato," it is the best place to begin, since the development of a true legato is often the first challenge for new organists.

It should be stated that the general principles of good piano hand position should be applied to modern organ technique. Fingers should be slightly curved, as they are when hands are at rest by your side. You may also grasp your knee and lift your hand, retaining the shape. Keep fingers close to keys as much as possible, never allowing the knuckles to "cave in." The wrist should remain relaxed, neither too high nor too low to guide and support the small yet fluid motions that are at the heart of a relaxed keyboard technique.

Legato Studies

a. Draw a clear 8' foundation stop such as the Principal and play, hands separately, then together, any major or minor scale. Listen carefully to each attack and release, making sure that there is a smooth connection between all notes.

b. On the same registration play the following finger substitution exercises separately, then together. Pass shorter fingers under the longer ones, longer ones over the shorter ones. Always count the beat's subdivision and dispel any tension you feel as soon as possible after the substitution, making sure fingers do not curl and the wrist has no excess tension.

c. Play the following legato studies, carefully observing all fingering, especially substitutions. Practice hands separately at first, choosing a practice tempo that allows you to play accurately in a relaxed manner. Using the metronome set to the eighth note can be helpful in mastering substitutions. These studies may be used as hymn introductions, as interludes between stanzas, or as brief preludes in the service. (See Legato hymn studies following.)

2. Non-legato or Détaché

Even the most reluctant of organists should be aware that there are two distinct approaches to organ technique that should have an impact on all who play the organ. Beginning in the nineteenth century and continuing in this century, organ and piano techniques began to share more common ground. The "basic touch" was legato, whether the music was written by Chopin or Vierne. In music of the fifteenth through eighteenth centuries, the "basic touch" was non-legato (sometimes called the articulated style, or détaché). This is not to say that either touch is exclusive to these periods; rather it indicates a basic approach to touch that the organist may use as a basis for exploring expressive possibilities communicated through articulation in music of all periods and styles.

3. Détaché Exercises

The following exercises and studies are designed to alert the organist to the many degrees of separation that are possible in an "articulated" style of playing. Practice these calmly, with fingers remaining close to the keys, and with the hand supported by a flexible and relaxed wrist. Practice with the metronome at first, counting aloud, making sure that rests are given full value. (See Détaché exercises following.)

B. Playing Hymns on the Manuals

Ask any church organist what the most challenging aspect of service playing is and the answer will probably be a resounding "hymn playing." Given the liturgical and spiritual importance of hymns, the wide variety of musical styles, and the difficulty of many pedal lines, beautiful, accurate, and convincing hymn playing is a challenge for *all* organists. If you find yourself in the position of having to produce a large number of hymns each week, you will probably elect to play them without pedal. The following guidelines for manuals-alone hymn playing represent one approach, though not the only approach, to simplifying hymns without sacrificing the essentials that produce good, rousing hymn playing. These ideas can and should be adapted as necessary for your situation.

At the outset it should be stated that hymn playing at the organ is basically legato. The soprano tune should always be played to imitate and support the vocal line—legato within the phrase yet repeating clearly all repeated notes. Further, major text punctuations should be reflected by an articulated silence (or "breath") in the tune and quite possibly other voices. For manuals-alone hymns, I suggest that as a rule, the alto, tenor, and bass be played legato with repeated notes tied. By following this rule, you will avoid sounding like a pianist playing hymns at the organ. Exceptions are always possible, as will be seen, but begin with strict observance of these rules and alter them as needed.

There are several recently published hymnals or hymn collections for manuals only listed in Appendix II. These will be helpful for your immediate use and can provide models of how you might simplify hymns from a standard hymnal. The guidelines, exercises, and sample hymns that follow should also get you started on the road to more confident hymn playing.

1. Photocopy hymns and service music each week so that you can mark scores thoroughly without being charged with defacing church property!*

2. Notice key and the meter; read the text. Mark the phrases and place a check or breath mark by soprano tune to indicate breathing at phrase endings. When this changes according to stanza, it should be so noted.

3. Play the tune in the legato fashion, yet observe all repeated notes.

4. Play the bass line (l.h.); play legato, tying all repeated notes unless bass note remains unchanged for more than one measure.

5. Play the soprano and bass together with the correct articulation.

6. Working slowly, phrase by phrase, mark fingerings as needed, keeping the alto, tenor, and bass legato with tied repeated notes. Be sure to detach soprano notes when needed without breaking the alto. (See Hymn exercises below.)

7. When awkward hand stretches occur, consider the following solutions: finger substitution; taking over the alto with the left hand or tenor with the right hand; omitting noncrucial chord tones such as a fifth, seventh, nonchord tone, or doubled note.

8. Breaths between phrases may be in soprano, the soprano and alto, or all four parts. Remember to sing and breathe with the congregation, keeping breaths generous and feeling the strong and weak beats.

9. The final chord should be played so that it leads to the next stanza without rhythmic uncertainty. In most cases, I suggest doubling the length of a last note, always leaving at least one beat for the preparational breath.

10. If more articulated accent is needed due to the number of singers, live acoustic, or the Sunday morning congregational "blahs," consider breaking more repeated bass notes to support the strong beats (e.g., break any repeated bass notes into beats one and three in 4/4 or into beat one in 3/4). (See Hymn studies following.)

---

*U.S. copyright law requires that permission to photocopy be obtained from owners of copyrighted music.

Ex. 1

Substituting on Subdivision of beat

Keep all fingers relaxed and resting on the keys at all times

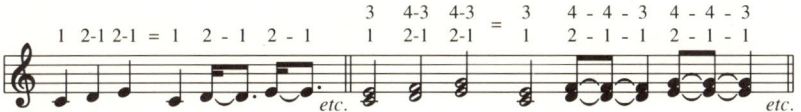

MUSIC: Janette Fishell
© 1996 Abingdon Press

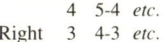
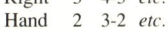

MUSIC: Jacques Lemmens
From *First Organ Book*. By permission of Wayne Leupold Editions.

MUSIC: Jacques Lemmens
From *First Organ Book*. By permission of Wayne Leupold Editions.

Ex. 2

Simultaneous Substitution of Two Fingers

Right Hand: *ascending*, substitute thumb first
descending, substitute 4th finger first

Left Hand: *ascending*, substitute 5th finger first
descending, substitute 2nd finger first

MUSIC: Janette Fishell
© 1996 Abingdon Press

This exercise should also be practiced beginning with Right Hand $\frac{4}{2}$ and Left Hand $\frac{2}{4}$

MUSIC: Jacques Lemmens
From *First Organ Book*. By permission of Wayne Leupold Editions.

MUSIC: Jacques Lemmens
From *First Organ Book*. By permission of Wayne Leupold Editions.

22

Ex. 3

Hymn Study on AZMON

Great: Principals 8' and 4'

sempre legato

MUSIC: Melody by Carl G. Gläser; arr. by Janette Fishell
Arr. © 1996 Abingdon Press

Ex. 4

Hymn Study on HANOVER

Great: Principals 8', 4', and 2'

MUSIC: Melody attr. to William Croft; arr. by Janette Fishell
Arr. © 1996 Abingdon Press

Ex. 5

Legato Hymn Study on HYMN TO JOY

RH: Trumpet 8'
LH: Principal 8'

*RH position should be close to sharps to facilitate "turning under."

MUSIC: Melody by Ludwig van Beethoven; arr. by Janette Fishell
Arr. © 1996 Abingdon Press

Ex. 6

Playing Legato Chords

The *impression* of legato can be maintained by keeping outer (lowest and highest) notes legato while breaking inner voices as needed. This reduces hand tension, which can develop when playing legato chordal passages.

For example:

MUSIC: Janette Fishell
© 1996 Abingdon Press

Ex. 7

Legato Hymn Study on LET US BREAK BREAD

Gt.   Principal 8', Sw to Gt 8'
Sw.   Flute 8', Flute Céleste 8', or Salicional 8', Voix Céleste 8'
Ped.   Soft 16' and 8'

*2-2 glissando, quickly slide the finger to the next key

MUSIC: African American spiritual; arr. by Janette Fishell
Arr. © 1996 Abingdon Press

Ex. 8

Legato Hymn Study on AMAZING GRACE

Sw.   Salicional 8', voix céleste 8'
Gt.   warm foundation 8'
Ped. soft 16' and 8'

MUSIC: 19th cent. USA melody; arr. by Janette Fishell
Arr. © 1996 Abingdon Press

Ex. 9

Détaché Exercises

Play with both hands.

(♪ = 120 - 208)

(♪ = 208) Feel the inner beat with precision!

Chords

(♪ = 120 - 208)

continue

Ex. 10

Right Hand Détaché Hymn Study on DUKE STREET

Patterns typical of 17th and 18th century articulation groupings.

RH Flutes 8' and 2'

MUSIC: Melody by John Hatton; arr. by Janette Fishell
Arr. © 1996 Abingdon Press

Ex. 11

The previous study could have been notated in the following manner. Practice this version,
matching the articulation of the previous notation.

MUSIC: Janette Fishell
© 1996 Abingdon Press

Ex. 12

Left Hand Détaché Hymn Study on
LASST UNS ERFREUEN

Principals 8', 4', 2'

*Thumb glissando, slide thumb quickly to the next note.

MUSIC: Melody from *Geistliche Kirchengesänge*; arr. by Janette Fishell
Arr. © 1996 Abingdon Press

Ex. 13

Détaché Hymn Study on IN DULCI JUBILO

Notice how the articulation reinforces the strong beat inflections, or accents, on 1 2 3 4 5 6.

RH   Flutes 8' and 2' or Flutes 8', 4', 2 2/3', 1 3/5'
LH   Cromhorn 8' or Principal 8'
     or both hands on Flute 4'

MUSIC: German melody; arr. by Janette Fishell
Arr. © 1996 Abingdon Press

Ex. 14

Hymn Soprano/Alto Exercises

When soprano moves to the same note previously found in alto, consider an "inner articulation" for melodic clarity.

is played:

* When alto moves to the same note previously found in soprano, approach without breaking since an articulative break is not needed for melodic clarity.

MUSIC: Janette Fishell
© 1996 Abingdon Press

is played:

Be careful to repeat all repeated notes in soprano while maintaining legato in alto.

MUSIC: Janette Fishell
© 1996 Abingdon Press

Ex. 15

Hymns Fingered and Adapted for Manuals Alone
OLD 100th

*Bass note repeats for rhythmic inflection.

WORDS: Thomas Ken
MUSIC: Attr. to Louis Bourgeois

Ex. 16

DIX

WORDS: Folliot S. Pierpoint
MUSIC: Conrad Kocher

* The final cadence may be lengthened in such a way that breathing space is present while the hymn's
  pulse remains constant.

Ex. 17

In the following hymn, many awkward doublings and nonessential chord tones have been omitted to facilitate a manuals-only performance. Compare this with the original to apppreciate the necessity of adaptation!

SINE NOMINE

WORDS: William W. How
MUSIC: Ralph Vaughan Williams

Ex. 17 (Cont.)

name, O Je - sus, be for - ev - er blest.

Al - le - lu - ia, Al - le - lu - ia!

Ex. 18

Gospel hymns with many repeated bass notes benefit from ties but consider breaking *bass only* for added rhythmic emphasis at intervals of 2 measures. In this example, all repeated note breaks are marked for half the value of the note (e.g. ♩♪ = ♪𝄾♪). After you gain control of repeated note technique, work for more subtlety by developing closer repeats as the music warrants (e.g. ♩♪ = ♪.𝄾♪).

SWEET HOUR

WORDS: William Walford
MUSIC: William B. Bradbury

* Soprano breaks for breath only during the second and third stanzas.

Ex. 19

Hymns with Pianistic Accompaniments
(Sustain chord root in bass.)
McGEE

Em - man - u - el, _____ Em - man - u - el, _____
_____ his name is called _____ Em - man - u - el. _____
God with us, _____ re - vealed in us, _____
_____ his name is called _____ Em - man - u - el.

WORDS & MUSIC: Bob McGee

Chapter Four
The Final Transition—
Building Pedal Technique

Exploring pedal technique for the first time is rather like swimming in cool water. Some people prefer to acclimate slowly, putting in one toe at a time, thereby adjusting to the water peacefully and calmly. Others throw caution to the wind and jump in, knowing that momentary discomfort will be rewarded by a wonderful sense of exhilaration. Whether you "dip in" one toe by adding an occasional pedal point or "jump into" more extensive pedal use, the following exercises, studies, and advice on hymn playing will help you make the final transition to becoming an organist.

A. Discovering Your "Comfort Zone"

It often takes students several lessons to find what I describe as the "comfort zone," that position on the bench that affords both stability and flexibility. Remember that while correct bench height is important in all organ playing, it is absolutely essential when one adds pedals. Review the information in chapter 1 concerning bench height and position before proceeding.

While they seldom flatter "haute couture" recital costumes, proper organ shoes are the second essential ingredient in the "comfort zone." Shoes must have a leather sole, be close-fitting (to aid maneuverability) and have an approximate one-inch heel to facilitate heel technique. (See Appendix III for some recommended shoes.)

B. Essential Pedal Aerobics

Before playing the following exercises and hymn studies, read these guidelines and memorize the "golden rules" of pedal technique found on page 42.

1. Pedaling is marked in the following manner:
    ∧ equals the toe   ∪ or O equals the heel
Either mark placed above the note indicates the right foot; placed
below the note, it indicates the left foot.
2. Most music is not marked, so eventually you must make and notate
pedaling choices. One general guideline is to choose pedaling that keeps
feet parallel to each other, touching when possible, heels together.
3. Organ music is usually notated on three staves, the lowest for
pedal, the middle for left hand, top for right. However, many times
hands share staves and often there are only two staves, as in a hymnal. When this is the case, the pedal usually plays the bass line and it
is *not* doubled by the left hand.
4. To read pedal octaves correctly, use this as a guide:

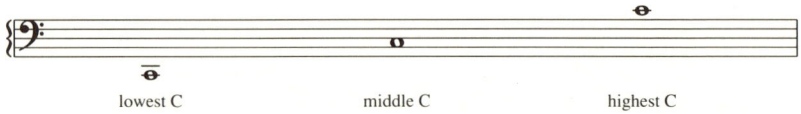

    lowest C   middle C   highest C

(See Essential Pedal Aerobics, Pedal Hymn Studies below).

C. Adding Pedal to Hymns

While manuals-alone hymn playing is a perfectly acceptable
option for the reluctant organist, at some point you will likely have
the undeniable urge to involve your feet in some way. When this day
arrives pat yourself on the back, for it means that you have become a
not-so-reluctant organist. Read on and incorporate these suggestions
at your own pace.

1. Adding Pedal Points

This is the technique of sustaining one note in the lowest register (in this case, literally the pedal), while changing harmonies
above it. This is the best way to begin using pedal in hymns and is
a useful technique for hymn variation even after one develops a
fluent pedal technique. Some guidelines for adding pedal points
follow.

a. Choose hymns with a simple chord vocabulary and slow harmonic rhythm (i.e., hymns with only a few chords that change relatively infrequently). Throughout this section we will use SPANISH HYMN as our example.

b. Identify the most important chord progressions, usually tonic, subdominant, and dominant. Pedal points will consist of the roots of these triads. (Note: there will frequently be a bit of dissonance between the manual chords and pedal points since the pedal notes change only with major chord progressions. Use your ears to judge whether the level of dissonance seems acceptable; if not, change pedals more frequently or choose a hymn with simpler harmonic vocabulary or slower chord changes.)

c. Circle the roots of these major chord progressions in the pedal (bass) line; change the octave placement when this is necessary to maintain your foot position.

d. Write out the bass pedal point progression underneath the staff.

e. Play the pedal line with legato connections between changing notes; you may "breathe" with the manuals at appropriate times such as phrase endings. Use good foot position with heels together within the compass of a fifth; knees and thighs remain relaxed.

f. Using roughly the same approach as in manuals-alone hymn playing, add soprano, alto and tenor voices. *Omit the bass line in the left hand.* This "frees" the left hand to assist the right more easily. (See the last measure of SPANISH HYMN.) (See SPANISH HYMN, exercise 31 below.)

2. Using Traditional Pedal Technique: An Introduction

Playing hymns with traditional pedal technique can call for quite advanced pedaling concepts. Do not be frustrated if you find this very difficult at first. Even the most talented organists have had to struggle at some point in their careers with hymn playing. However, over time, certain techniques do become more automatic as you gain experience in reading the bass line with your pedal and you see patterns emerge from the black dots on the page.

Choose a brief, relatively easy hymn in a key with no more than one accidental. Using the rules below, mark it and practice it like an etude, not like a hymn that you must play this coming Sunday! Allow it to develop and "settle" technically before you play it in a service. Remember to practice the pedal alone, pedal and left hand, pedal and right hand, and hands alone, with metronome to the eighth note. Play the complete bass line in the pedal without doubling it in the left hand, as this is unnecessary and inhibits your control of the manuals.

The Golden Rules of Pedal Technique

1. Keep legs (including knees) relaxed, feet touching. While many technique manuals emphasize "knees together," I feel this can cause lower back and leg tension, which inhibits a truly free technique. I recommend knees stay relaxed, not awkwardly splayed but nearly touching, and feet touching whenever possible.

2. Keep heels together within the compass of a fifth. Feet work like a fan, opening for larger intervals, closing for smaller ones. This is the best method of interval measurement. (See Diagram 2 on page 44.)

3. Play on the inside or ball of foot, never on the outside edge.

4. Play pedals with a firm and rhythmically decisive ankle action, but without any excess energy or leg motion. Check relaxation in the following manner: When toes play, heels remain relaxed, not raised. The same is true of the toes when the heels play.

5. Play as close to the black pedal keys as possible at all times.

6. Strive to prepare and play pedals without looking at feet or "feeling" for the sharps.

Rules for Hymn Articulation

This is certainly not the only approach, but it is one that results in clear, lyrical, and rhythmic hymn playing. While the rules may be relaxed later, follow them scrupulously when you begin.

1. Play all voices legato with the following exceptions: Soprano and bass will break into all repeated notes; alto and tenor will tie repeated notes, breaking into strong beats only (in 3/4 hymns, break into the first beat only; in 4/4 hymns, break into beats one and three; in 6/8 hymns, break into the first and second big beat).

2. Punctuation and congregational breaths should be reflected in your articulation. Breathe (break) with soprano, and perhaps one or all other voices, at internal phrases when there is punctuation. Be careful to reflect each stanza's text in your punctuation (if only in the soprano). When stanzas vary, mark your score to indicate when you break and when you carry through.

3. Sometimes it is preferable to add a half or complete measure between stanzas to keep the inner beat constant and predictable. This also allows for sufficient breathing space between stanzas while it maintains the hymn's pulse.

4. Sing the hymn while playing in order to reflect the text better and to feel the shape of the musical line. Alternatively you can sing on a syllable such as "loo" or, especially in very long hymns, the number of the stanza. This also can help you remember which stanza you are playing!

5. As with all rules, there are possible exceptions that are presented in almost any hymn. When, as in many gospel hymns, strictly following the rules results in too many complete chordal breaks, consider tying any voice except the melody. More space between repeated notes and phrases is needed in an acoustically "live" room or when leading a large number of singers; less is necessary in a "dry" room. The overall rule is, as in all music, use your ears! Record services to ensure that your approach to hymn playing is working.

Diagram 2

Keep heels together, feet touching.

Within the compass of a 5th, feet act like a fan; open for larger intervals, closes together for smaller intervals.

When playing a 2nd, one foot will move back slightly while the other moves up.

playing a 5th

playing a 3rd

playing a 2nd with left back
right up

playing a 2nd with left up
right back

Two hymns, CANONBURY and HURSLEY (see examples following), have more articulation marks than is advisable merely to clarify the rules. And while no fingering has been marked, most hymns will require some fingering, especially when you take the alto voice with the left hand. A "cleaner" copy of OLD 100th is included to show how you might begin to mark your hymns. See chapter 6 for more advice on hymn-playing techniques.

Ex. 20

Hymn Articulation

Repeated alto and tenor notes

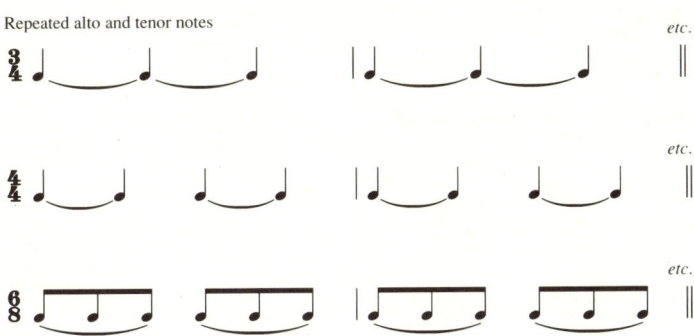

Ex. 21-A

Essential Pedal Aerobics
Legato and Détaché Exercise for All Toes

Ped. Principal 8' or 4'

heels together

*When feet play a second, one foot moves slightly back (∧), the other forward (∧̄). Regain normal position after seconds are complete.

MUSIC: Janette Fishell
© 1996 Abingdon Press

Ex. 21-B

MUSIC: Janette Fishell
© 1996 Abingdon Press

Ex. 21-C

∧ etc.   ∧   ∧

                    normal
                    position

MUSIC: Janette Fishell
© 1996 Abingdon Press

Ex. 21-D

∧   ∧

MUSIC: Janette Fishell
© 1996 Abingdon Press

Ex. 21-E

Pivoting: When moving to the top or the bottom of the pedal board you will need to reposition slightly by *pivoting*. Keep knees parallel and turn them slightly to the *left* when descending, to the *right* when ascending. Pivot by gently pushing into the desired position with the *right foot* when descending, the left when ascending.

↓ *pivot left!*   *pivot left!*
                         ↓∧

∧

MUSIC: Janette Fishell
© 1996 Abingdon Press

Ex. 21-F

pivot right   *pivot right*
↓   ↓

MUSIC: Janette Fishell
© 1996 Abingdon Press

Ex. 22-A

Heel/Toe Exercises

Remember to keep legs, especially knees, relaxed! Play from the ankle, using the *least* amount of energy possible.

MUSIC: Janette Fishell
© 1996 Abingdon Press

Ex. 22-B

Repeat the exercise with right foot.

MUSIC: Janette Fishell
© 1996 Abingdon Press

Ex. 22-C

Larger Intervals with One Foot (knees stay relaxed and may open *slightly*)

MUSIC: Janette Fishell
© 1996 Abingdon Press

Ex. 22-D

Substitution with One Foot

MUSIC: Janette Fishell
© 1996 Abingdon Press

Ex. 22-E

Substitution Between Feet

Performed:

MUSIC: Janette Fishell
© Copyright 1996 Abingdon Press

Ex. 23

Pedal Hymn Studies
Alternate Toe Study on AZMON

Ped.: Principals 16', 8', 4'

Bring out right foot melody by lengthening note, not by playing the key harder.

MUSIC: Melody by Carl G. Gläser; arr. by Janette Fishell
Arr. © 1996 Abingdon Press

Ex. 24

Heel/Toe Study on GLORIA

Ped.: Principals 8', 4'

MUSIC: French carol melody; arr. Janette Fishell
Arr. © 1996 Abingdon Press

Ex. 25

Heel/Toe Study on OLD 100th

Ped.: Principals 8', 4', 4' (mixture, reed)

MUSIC: Melody attr. to Louis Bourgeois; arr. by Janette Fishell
Arr. © 1996 Abingdon Press

Ex. 26

Manual/Pedal Study on CONDITOR ALME

LH: Principal 8'
Ped: Soft 16' and 8'

MUSIC: Plainsong; arr. by Janette Fishell
Arr. © 1996 Abingdon Press

Ex. 27

Manual/Pedal Hymn Study on MIGHTY SAVIOR

Hands: Flute 8' and tremulant
Ped: Flute 4'

Tenderly (sempre legato)

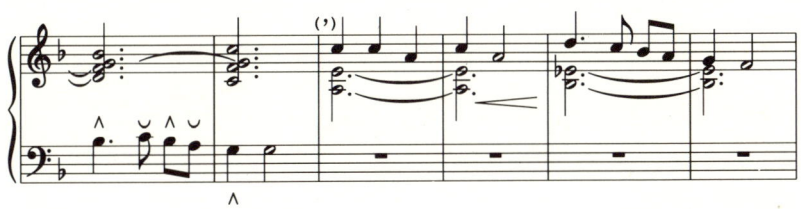

MUSIC: Melody by David Hurd; arr. by Janette Fishell
© 1985, 1996 G.I.A. Publications, Inc.

Manual/Pedal Hymn Study on THE CALL

Ex. 28

RH: Warm solo stops
LH: Flute 8' or string plus céleste
Ped.: Soft 16' and 8'

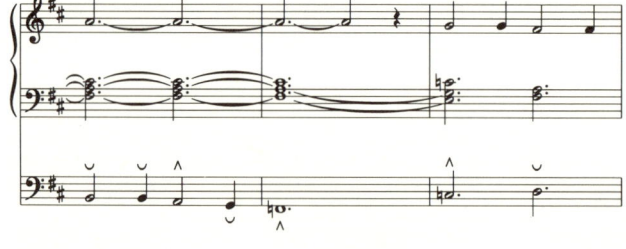

MUSIC: Melody by Ralph Vaughan Williams; arr. by Janette Fishell
Arr. © 1996 Abingdon Press

Ex. 29

Manual/Pedal Hymn Study on LORD OF THE DANCE

RH: Flutes 8', (2 2/3'), 2'
LH: Flute 8', (4')
Ped.: Princ. 8'

Sprightly and détaché

Ex. 30

Manual/Pedal Study on LOBE DEN HERREN

Marcato (*subtle détaché throughout*)

*Feel the "weight" of the strong or inflected beats, the lightness of the weak beats.

MUSIC: Melody from *Erneuerten Gesangbuch;* arr. by Janette Fishell
Arr. © 1996 Abingdon Press

Ex. 31

SPANISH HYMN

WORDS: Christian Henry Bateman
MUSIC: Trad. melody; arr. by Benjamin Carr; harm. by Austin C. Lovelace
Harm. © 1964 Abingdon Press

Ex. 32

4/4 Hymn Marked According to Rules

Slurs (⌒) indicate legato touch *or* ties; dotted slurs (⌐) indicate an articulation that varies according to stanza.

CANONBURY

1. Lord, speak to me, that I may speak in
2. O strength - en me, that while I stand firm
3. O teach me, Lord, that I may teach the
4. O fill me with thy full - ness, Lord, un -
5. O use me, Lord, use e - ven me, just

liv - ing ech - oes of thy tone; as thou hast sought, so
on the rock, and strong in thee, I may stretch out a
pre - cious things thou dost im - part; and wing my words, that
til my ver - y heart o'er - flow in kin - dling thought and
as thou wilt, and when, and where, un - til thy bless - ed

let me seek thine err - ing chil - dren lost and lone.
lov - ing hand to wres - tlers with the trou - bled sea.
they may reach the hid - den depths of many a heart.
glow - ing word, thy love to tell, thy praise to show.
face I see, thy rest, thy joy, thy glo - ry share.

LH plays alto to facilitate legato.
WORDS: Frances R. Havergal
MUSIC: Adapt. from Robert Schumann

Ex. 33

When following the rules strictly results in completely breaking the entire chord (as in measures 1-2), you may wish to tie the alto, tenor, and/or bass.

HURSLEY

Break Sop St. 1-4

1. Come, sin - ners,   to   the   gos - pel   feast,   let   ev - ery
2. See him set   forth   be - fore   your   eyes;   be - hold   the
3. Ye who be - lieve   his   rec - ord   true   shall   sup   with

ossia

etc. *When bass lines have a great number of repeated notes, you may wish to tie, breaking only into the strong beats.*

soul   be   Je - sus' guest.   Ye   need   not   one   be
bleed - ing   sac - ri - fice;   his   of - fered   love   make
him   and   he   with   you;   come   to   the   feast,   be

left   be - hind,   for God hath   bid   all   hu - man - kind.
haste to em - brace,   and free - ly   now   be   saved   by   grace.
saved   from sin,   for Je - sus   waits   to   take   you   in.

WORDS: Charles Wesley
MUSIC: *Katholisches Gesangbuch,* ca. 1774; adapt. from *Metrical Psalter,* 1855

*An "inner articulation" played:

Ex. 34

OLD 100th

Praise God, from whom all bless - ings flow; praise him, all crea-tures here be - low; praise him a - bove, ye heaven - ly host; praise Fa - ther, Son, and Ho - ly Ghost. A - men.

Pedal may also slur or tie into "Amen"

A - men.   *or*   A - men.

WORDS: Thomas Ken
MUSIC: Attr. to Louis Bourgeois

Chapter Five
Playing Accompaniments Musically and Idiomatically

Keep one eye on the score, the other in the mirror.

When faced with playing accompaniments, many reluctant organists will choose to use the piano. While this is often a good option, many times it is impractical or impossible. The following concepts of score adaptation and registration are offered as general guidelines that can assist you in playing more idiomatic accompaniments. Some of the same concepts can be used occasionally in organ repertoire as well.

A. Score Adaptation

The art of accompanying on the organ is knowing both what to leave out and what to put in. Most pianistic accompaniments need both simplifying and augmenting to sound idiomatic on the organ. Even accompaniments written for the organ can often benefit from similar adaptation. With experience many of the following techniques come naturally but, until then, mark your score well to indicate the necessary changes.

1. While still maintaining a sense of motion, which is present in the original figuration, adapt arpeggios, repeated notes or chords, and tremolos by tying selected notes or converting figuration into chords. (See Examples 35-37.)

2. Thick chords may be "thinned" by eliminating doubled notes or chords. (See Example 38.)

3. Extremes in range may be changed to aid clarity or avoid sounding too harsh or bright. (See Example 39.)

4. Add chordal support when texture seems empty without it. Identify and sustain chord roots and play as pedal points.

(See Examples 40 and 41.)

5. Finger difficult passages that require legato touch using the concepts discussed in chapter 3, such as finger substitution. (See Example 42; Examples 43 and 44 organ accompaniments that require adaptation.)

B. Registration

Accompanying is also the art of recognizing the role or roles the organ plays. Answer the following questions before you decide on registration for an accompaniment. Does the organ merely double the voice parts or provide a quiet background? Does it provide more solid foundational reinforcement and have independent material such as introductions and interludes? Is there material that should be played with a solo color on a separate manual? Once the score is understood, you should begin to experiment with registrations. Remember the following guidelines in choosing appropriate colors.

1. Strive to achieve balanced dynamics with the choir or soloist.

An effective accompaniment should provide necessary support without overwhelming the choir or soloist. I suggest playing accompaniments on an enclosed division (such as the Swell) for maximum dynamic flexibility since unenclosed divisions (such as the Great) cannot be made softer with as much speed or subtlety. However, you may wish to move to the Great, which will invariably be coupled to the Swell, when accompanying large forces, for climactic sections or louder accompaniments, or for organ solo passages.

There are two ways of changing dynamics at the organ: opening or closing the expression pedal or pedals, and adding or subtracting stops. You will need to become somewhat adept at both techniques since they are critical to achieving proper dynamic balance.

a. **The Expression Pedal**

Mark *crescendi* and *diminuendi* with a highlighter. Open and close the expression pedal as needed, "feeling" or preferably singing the *crescendo* or *diminuendo,* rather than "thinking" it. In other words, feel the dynamic as you do at the piano, allowing the change to be part of the music rather than just a physical command. You may write a note in the score such as "prepare right foot on swell pedal" until it becomes an automatic response. Avoid "riding the swell" (i.e., incessantly opening and closing the swell pedal), as this produces symptoms akin to seasickness in your listeners.

b. **Adding or Subtracting Stops**

Grade the Swell divisional pistons (or general pistons when divisional pistons are absent) according to the general guidelines in chapter 2 and below. This results in a palette of soft foundations through the full Swell, the dynamics of which are controlled by the swell pedal. By coupling Swell to the Great foundation 8' (and 4'), a more forceful option is instantly available. For changes, press the piston at appropriate phrase endings, breathing with at least one part of the accompaniment. Sometimes it is effective to add or subtract stops while the choral or solo line is still present rather than before their rests, as this provides a seamless dynamic change. (See Example 45.)

2. Choose appropriate timbres and pitch levels.

Apart from dynamic balance, your choices of timbre and pitch level are important, for these affect the tone and blend of those you accompany. Even if dynamics balance, too much upper work can result in a strident tone from both organ and choir or soloist. Conversely, registrations that are muddy (the result of too many 8' or 16' and 8' foundations) lack rhythmic incisiveness and can result in a lethargic, flat choral or solo performance.

Your choice should also take into account the musical style of the accompaniment. Is it slow and sustained or fast and strongly rhythmic? Style is also related to the music's historical period. Choose registrations that reinforce the sound ideals summarized below:

Baroque/Classical (or Contemporary Anthems in Neo-Baroque or Neo-Classical Style)	**Characteristic 19th and 20th Century**
Register for clarity	Register for homogeneity
Terraced dynamics	Gradual dynamic changes

Smaller range of dynamic variation	Dramatic variation in dynamics
Typical touch is non-legato with legato for expressive, slower pieces	Typical touch is legato with non-legato used for clarity and to imitate orchestral effects
Only infrequent and simple stop changes; no pistons on organ	Registration changes can be frequent and dramatic depending on the music's mood and dynamic: pistons will be used
No swell box was used	Swell box assists in dynamic changes

a. **Pre-Nineteenth-Century Accompaniments**

When accompanying music by composers such as Bach, Handel, Purcell, Haydn, or Mozart, you should keep the following guidelines in mind. Registrations are simpler, consisting of one- to three-stop combinations that emphasize clarity. Dynamics are terraced, with few gradual changes. You may change manuals and add or subtract stops for dynamic change, but do not use the swell box as this was foreign to the period. Do not use the céleste, but you may use the tremulant. (This is especially good with the Flute 8'.) Most stop changes should be simple and achieved by hand rather than by piston since organs of this period did not have pistons. Remember that the basic touch is non-legato, especially in faster, highly rhythmic pieces. Do not tie yourself in knots keeping figuration legato when a crisper, non-legato touch is called for. (See chapter 3, page 18, to review non-legato touch.)

Accompaniments in modern editions of Baroque music most often consist of a bass line and chordal framework based on the original continuo or figured bass part. Other editions of Baroque works add to the continuo some or all of the original instrumental parts. Example 46, "Alleluia, O Come and Praise the Lord," by

J. S. Bach, is an example of a modern edition with a realization of the continuo as its accompaniment. There are at least three interesting ways to register this piece.

1. Play it on the manuals with Swell Flutes 8' and 4' for the *mezzo piano* sections, and Great Principal 8' and 4' for the *mezzo forte* sections.

2. If you have a 16' Flute or Principal in the manuals, play the bass line on a separate manual using 16' and 8' or 16' and 4' foundations; play right hand chords on Flutes 8' and 4'.

3. Play the bass line in the pedal with 16' and 8' or 8' only, using Swell Flutes 8' and 4' for the *mezzo piano,* and Great Principal 8' and 4' for the *mezzo forte.* (See Example 46.)

"Gloria," from Vivaldi's *Magnificat,* is an example of a combination continuo and instrumental part accompaniment. (See Example 47.)

b. **Nineteenth- and Twentieth-Century Accompaniments**

For most nineteenth- and twentieth-century anthem or solo accompaniments, follow the suggested swell gradations outlined below, adjusting them as necessary. While there is some disagreement among organists, I think the judicious use of the céleste (always with its "partner") can be very effective when not overused. The céleste should not be used in music composed before the Romantic period (before approximately 1825), as it is not characteristic of organ tone of this time.

POSSIBLE SWELL GRADATIONS FOR ACCOMPANYING				
SWELL ①	SWELL ②	SWELL ③	SWELL ④	SWELL ⑤
Flute 8' (+ Tremolo?) OR: Salicional 8' + Voix Céleste 8'	Flute 8', Salicional 8', or Gemshorn 8' + Flute 4' (- tremolo)	Swell ② + Principal 4' (Flute 2')	Swell ③ + Oboe 8' or Trumpet 8'	Swell ④ + Mixture
GREAT:	Principal 8' (+ Principal 4' or Flute 4') and the Swell to Great 8'			
PEDAL:	16' and 8' foundations to balance the hands Couplers Swell to Pedal and Great to Pedal may be used			

63

Play on the Swell, moving to the Great for louder introductions, interludes, or climactic passages. When hands are on the Great, you may need to add the Great to Pedal by hand or with a reversible toe stud so that the Pedal balances with the hands. When appropriate, play solo melodies on another manual either by having the registration "set up" from the beginning, or by setting a general piston. Solo color choices are varied but should be chosen to support and maintain the overall character of the piece. Some solo choices for broad, lyrical, expressive and warm melodies are Flute 8'; Principal 8' + Flute 8'; Oboe 8'; Flute + Nazard 2 ⅔'. All the solo colors may be used with the tremulant. For fast, rhythmic, buoyant or brighter melodies, several choices are Flute 8' + 2'; a mutation complex such as the Cornet; or Trumpet 8'.

C. Other Considerations

1. Choral accompanying always carries with it the responsibility of being ready to play all voice parts as needed. Learn to shift as necessary between voice parts and accompaniment as choirs have been known to need help on Sunday morning!

2. Mark all breaths and dynamics as confirmed by the conductor or soloist. Usually it is most effective when at least one voice in the accompaniment breathes along with the choral parts; judge by the importance of the cadence and the room's acoustic how much the accompaniment should break.

3. When playing Baroque accompaniments, beware of phrase marks, articulations, manual changes, dynamics, registrations, tempo markings, and even pedal lines, which the editor might have added to the original. Remember that pedals are often optional and the overall approach to touch is non-legato.

4. Tasteful ornamentation in Baroque accompaniments is appropriate. Always listen for ornamentation a soloist may include, and experiment with your own, at least adding trills at the cadence. (Important rule of thumb: begin trills on the dissonant note, whether it is the upper or the lower.)

Ex. 35

"Alleluia" from *Mount of Olives*
(Beethoven)

can be played:

Ex. 36

"Hear, O Lord" from *Christus*
(Mendelssohn)

Ex. 36 (Cont.)

can be played:

MUSIC: Arr. by Hal H. Hopson

Ex. 37

"Gloria"
(Haydn)

can be played:

"Alleluia"
(Beethoven)

can be played:

Ex. 39

"Let Joyful Anthems Rise"
(Handel)

can be played:

Using the Principal 8' and 4' provides an octave doubling; see page 62 for discussion of articulation in Baroque accompaniments.

Ex. 40

"Lord, You're My Shepherd"

WORDS: Susan Eltringham, based on Psalm 23
MUSIC: DETROIT; arr. by Susan Eltringham

Ex. 40 (Cont.)

may be played:

Swell: Soft 8′
Great: Solo flute 8′
Pedal: Soft 16′ and 8′

Play solo line on an appropriate solo stop if no solo instrument is used.

Add Pedal and harmonic roots, and sustain consonant notes for a fuller harmonic texture.

1. Lord, you're my shep herd I will trust in you, I
2. You give me strength that's new each day, you

WORDS: Susan Eltringham, based on Psalm 23
MUSIC: DETROIT; arr. by Susan Eltringham

© 1995 Abingdon Press

Ex. 41

"Gloria"
(Haydn)

can be played:

Ex. 42

"My Song Shall be Always of the Loving-kindness"
(Sampson)

The "illusion" of legato is achieved by keeping the lowest L.H. voices legato;
fingering is learned faster if patterns repeat.

Used by permission of Novello and Co., Ltd.

Ex. 43

"The First Word" from
The Seven Last Words of Christ
(Dubois)

can be played:

Ex. 44

"The Third Word" from
The Seven Last Words of Christ
(Dubois)

can be played:

RH Solo stop: Principal 8', Oboe 8', or Flute 8'

"Introit-Kyrie" from *Requiem*
(Fauré)

MUSIC: Arr. by John Rutter
Used by permission of Hinshaw Music, Inc.

Ex. 46   **"Alleluia, O Come and Praise the Lord"**
          (Bach)

Performance notes: Use détaché touch between most (♩) beats; you may choose to group, or "slur," patterns within the (♩) beat.

♩ / ♩ / ♩   but   ♩. ⌣ ♩ / ♩

Inflect the first beat (the *strong* beat) by feeling more rhythmic "weight" behind it. The measure should feel the "swing" of **1** 2 3.

Ex. 47

Vivaldi "Gloria" from *Magnificat*

Allegro

can be played:

Performance note: Same détaché concepts as in Example 12 (break between ♩ beat). *Play LH bass line as transcribed (down the octave) if you have no manual 16'. If you have manual 16', then play in original octave on a separate manual.

Chapter Six
The "Compleat" Organist

B y this point in the book, I hope that you have begun to consider yourself a "new and improving" organist rather than a reluctant one! The information below addresses some of the most common questions I encounter among new organists. Because of limited space, there are many issues that can only be touched on. I recommend Appendixes II and III, which list many helpful resources that can lead to the next step in your development as a church musician.

A. More About Hymn Playing

1. Tempo

As with all music, any hymn can thrive at a range of tempi. Here are some guidelines to help you find a successful tempo for each hymn.

a. Determine the mood of text and the style of the tune. Is the text joyful, meditative, or penitential? Is the tune strongly rhythmic, broad, ceremonial, or folklike? What is the key? Is it minor but with triumphant text? Is it a major key with penitential or reflective text? Does the harmony change frequently, as in a Lutheran chorale, adding "weight" to tempo?

b. Find the tune's "big" (or strong) beats using the following:

$$4/4 \text{ or } 6/8 = \text{in "2"}$$
$$3/4 = \text{in "1"}$$

Sing the hymn while conducting the big beat, feeling the natural "swing" of the music as it moves between inflections. Sense the "lightness" of the weak beats; do not allow them to sound as accented as the big beat.

c. Sing, play, and record the hymn, feeling big beat inflections and breathing generously at phrase endings and between stanzas.

d. Evaluate the effectiveness of your tempo and metrical shaping. Can you hear a circular motion that travels from downbeat to downbeat? If the natural swing of the measure is disturbed, is it stopped by artificial pauses or cheated by a rushed beat?

e. External conditions may affect your tempo. Play more broadly when you have a reverberant acoustic, large congregation, unfamiliar hymn, or when you change harmony with a free accompaniment (see below). Often a fast tempo assists in dry acoustics. You should also be sensitive to the mood of the service, both in tempo and registration.

2. Playing "Amens"

"Amens" should be played in the same spirit as the hymn. It should be an assured "So be it!" rather than an apologetic "It's over." For musical continuity, try tying a common tone or the pedal from the final hymn chord; never reduce the volume since this weakens the statement.

3. Effective Hymn Registrations

These can be built using the graded piston principle explained in chapter 2. Colors should be based on the Great Principal chorus with reinforcement from the Swell and Choir. Pedal should balance the manuals and remain uncoupled to the Great if possible. Once you are comfortable with the hymn, plan to change registration between most stanzas, reflecting the text when possible. The following is an over-simplification, but provides a possible model:

STANZA	TEXT MOOD	SUGGESTED REGISTRATION
1.	Joyful	Foundations 8', 4', 2', Mixture
2.	More reflective	Foundations 8', 4', (2')
3.	Darker, perhaps speaking of sin	Foundations 8', 4', Reed 8'
4.	Triumphant	Foundations 8', 4', 2', Mixture, Reeds

When you have developed your pedal technique sufficiently, solo the right-hand tune on a Cornet or Trumpet 8' (perhaps reinforced with other foundation stops) and accompany with left hand and pedal.

4. Playing Introductions

Introductions may consist of the entire hymn, the first and last phrases, or just a refrain. Vary your introductions by sometimes beginning with the tune alone (as written, down the octave, or even in the pedal!) or the tune in hands over a pedal point. You can also play the tune in canon (right hand/left hand) on two different colors, such as a Principal against a soft reed. When using these ideas for more creative introductions, I suggest ending with the final phrase as written in the hymnal with a fuller foundation-based registration as a signal to the congregation that it is time to sing. (See Examples 48 and 49.)

5. Free Accompaniments

When played well, free accompaniments can lift congregational singing to new heights; when poorly played, they can impede the most important musical aspect of the service. When playing them, practice them diligently and use them sparingly at first.

Traditionally used on final stanzas of one or two hymns per service, reharmonizations should always clearly maintain rhythmic pulse, tune, and key. I recommend printing "sing in unison on final stanza" in the service bulletin to avoid confusion and harmonic clashes.

a. Play free accompaniments only on tunes that are well known to your congregation.

b. Play more broadly and more articulately than you played the rest of the hymn to assist singers in feeling the pulse and singing the tune despite any harmonic changes.

c. Make sure your accompaniment doesn't clash with the tune.

d. Feel free to simplify a free accompaniment (e.g., by leaving out "busy" pedal lines).

e. To ensure that the congregation doesn't immediately get lost or give up, begin the first stanza with one or two beats on the unison tune, then go into the free accompaniment.

f. You may use only part of a free accompaniment by beginning the last stanza as printed in the hymnal and moving to the free accompaniment on the third phrase.

6. Playing Interludes

Interludes, especially when needed to lengthen processions, are wonderful ways to vary hymns. You can use all or part of a free accompaniment as an interlude, write your own, or repeat part of the hymn, with or without variation.

a. Interludes must maintain the character, pulse, and key of the hymn.

b. To avoid confusion, they should begin on the final measure while the congregation is still singing the last notes of the hymn.

c. They should last at least eight measures (usually two phrase lengths) and end clearly either on the tonic or the dominant. Rehearse with your choir to ensure that they will enter on time, thereby supporting the congregation.

d. An interlude may be skillfully and tastefully used to modulate up one half or one whole step. Modulations should avoid jarring shifts or theatrical effects. When modulating up one step, a common-chord or common-tone modulation is effective. Identify chords for the keys in question in the following manner:

C major going to D major:	The common chords are E minor and G major.
	The altered chords that can be useful are D minor and A minor.

A half-step modulation is more challenging because there is only one common tone between keys related by semi-tone. One possible formula, suggested by Max Miller in his article, "A First Step in Keyboard Modulation," *The American Organist* (October, 1982), follows, illustrated in C major.

C major going to D♭ major		C major triad→	F minor→	A♭ major→	D♭
	in C	I	iv	-	-
	in D♭	-	iii	V	I

After arriving in the new key, you may conclude by playing the final phrase of the hymn. Bring the interlude to its conclusion with a clear cadence on either the new tonic or dominant. (See Example 50.)

B. Listening and Responding to the Service

The difference between an adequate and a wonderful service player is that the latter understands the mood of the service and, through registration, tempo, and musical selections, "pulls" the congregation further into the community that good liturgy should build. While much of this is or becomes instinctive, there are some techniques that beginning organists can explore that will help transform the service.

1. The Voluntaries (Prelude, Offertory, Postlude)

When playing the service prelude, the organist actually becomes the first worship leader of the hour. The prelude, and all of the day's voluntaries, should be carefully chosen to reflect the theme or mood of the service, scripture, and/or hymn choices. Titles should be printed in the service bulletin so the congregation can see the connection between voluntaries and service theme.

If you have trouble with "preservice chatter," work with your minister to teach the congregation that the opening voluntary is not preservice "Musak," but is a carefully integrated part of the worship service. Just as they do not talk during the scripture reading, hymns, or sermon, they should not do so during the opening music. Try including singers or instrumentalists periodically in your voluntaries as another way of capturing the congregation's attention.

Organ offertories usually need to be brief and are often quiet or reflective. If you sing a hymn after the offertory, try to play a voluntary on that hymn tune whenever possible. It is very effective if a modulatory bridge to the Doxology or other presentation music is played, linking the offertory to the congregational response. (See Max Miller's article cited above for more ideas regarding modulation.)

Postludes provide the one opportunity to play louder, more virtuosic music. After an hour's service, postludes that are too brief seem anticlimactic. Lengthen short postludes by repeating them with a different registration.

2. Registration

Nothing can destroy the reflective mood of a service more quickly than organ playing that is too loud or too fast! Conversely, a joyous and energized worship service can be stopped dead in its tracks by inappropriately penitential, somber organ voluntaries, or dull, colorless registrations. Here it is helpful to differentiate between the moods set by processional and recessional hymns and internal hymns such as those between scripture readings, after the offertory, or during Communion. The former generally need powerful registrations and forceful introductions, while the latter may benefit from quieter introductions, especially if they come at a more introspective moment of the service.

3. Common music

Thank heaven (literally) that most denominations now observe in Communion the true spirit of *Eucharistia,* which means "thanksgiving." While loud, bombastic music is inappropriate, music that conveys the joy inherent in the word *thanksgiving* is called for. Playing voluntaries on communion hymns, either alone or in conjunction with the singing of the hymn, is most appropriate. Another wonderful idea is to "bring back" themes from other music of the day (hymns, a melody from the day's anthem, even service music). This can help tie together the service in a very meaningful way.

4. Silence

Sometimes we can help our congregations hear the voice of God best by intentionally allowing silence to be part of the worship. Consider an occasional silent Communion, a silent time of worship preparation (no prelude), or silent reflection after the service (no postlude). These ideas are especially effective during Lent. The sounds of a baby crying, birds singing, or rain on the roof are all eloquent manifestations of God among us. Don't feel that you need to cover them with "interludes"—especially ones that are trite or uninteresting. When bridges or interludes are needed within the service, try to base them on previous or upcoming hymns, the anthem, or other meaningful music of the day.

C. Beyond Sunday Morning—Ideas for Other Occasions

1. Weddings

Consider making a tape that can be given to brides containing a variety of processions, preservice music, and solos. This can save much time in the planning process. Work with your minister and music committee to develop and distribute wedding music guidelines that clearly state any policies your church has regarding music selection. Emphasize to the bridal couple your responsibility to provide music that is appropriate for the worship service as well as beautiful. Consider the use of hymns (either as processions or in the service) since congregational singing is a hallmark of Protestant worship.

2. Funerals or Memorial Services

As with Communion, many churches have changed the focus in funerals or memorial services from a death-centered sadness to resurrection-centered triumph. Many families will request favorite hymns such as "Amazing Grace," "Now Thank We All Our God," "A Mighty Fortress Is Our God," or "Abide with Me," and it is good to learn voluntaries on these and other favorite memorial hymns so that you are prepared to play them at short notice. A simple yet very moving postlude to a memorial service is the hymn "A Mighty Fortress Is Our God" played forcefully and triumphantly. See Appendix II for further suggestions about service music.

Ex. 48

God Rest Ye Merry Gentlemen

Introduction using canon, pedal point, ending with hymn's final phrase.

RH: Reed 8'
LH: Princ. 8'
Ped.: Flutes 16', 8', 4'

MUSIC: 18th cent. English carol melody; arr. Janette Fishell
Arr. © 1996 Abingdon Press

Ex. 48 (Cont.)

Good Christian Friends, Rejoice

Hymn introduction using deocrated tune in bicinium style; hymn is shortened but last phrase returns to fuller chordal texture on one manual.

Swell: Flutes 8' and 2'
Great: Principal 8', 4', 2'

MUSIC: German melody; arr. by Janette Fishell
Arr. © 1996 Abingdon Press

Ex. 50

Come Down, O Love Divine

Hymn modulation using formulas from Max Miller's article.

Modulation up one-half step (flat side)

Modulation up one whole step (sharp side)

MUSIC: Ralph Vaughan Williams

Postlude

So now you know the truth about playing the organ. You know that it takes disciplined practice, patience, and a sense of humor when your hands and feet clearly do not wish to cooperate. But persevere! Every minute you spend becoming a better organist is one more minute you give back your talent in service to God. It is important to remember that God demands not perfection but commitment to whatever is our best at any given moment. And by following the ideas in this book, your personal best *will* improve steadily!

Some Sunday mornings when I have a difficult time finding inspiration for the day's services, I recall the following lines from one of my favorite hymns. These words always call me to serve God with a truly joyful spirit. I hope that they will lighten your path on the Sundays to come.

Awake, awake to love and work!
The lark is in the sky,
the fields are wet with diamond dew,
the worlds awake to cry
their blessings on the Lord of life,
as he goes meekly by.

To give and give, and give again,
what God hath given thee;
to spend thyself nor count the cost;
to serve right gloriously
the God who gave all worlds that are,
and all that are to be.

No. 9, stanzas 4, 6
The Hymnal 1982 (Episcopal)
Geoffrey Anketel Studdert-Kennedy
(1883–1929)

Appendix I
Glossary

Baroque: The period in music history dating from the latter part of the seventeenth century to approximately 1750. Many post-1930 composers have written in styles that may be described as neo-Baroque as seen in their preference for forms and registrations more characteristic of North German music of the seventeenth and eighteenth centuries.

Basso continuo (b.c.): Also called continuo, figured bass, or thorough bass. A Baroque method of keyboard accompaniment in which the notated bass line is augmented by usually improvised, chordal support. Typically, basso continuo was performed by two instruments: an organ or harpsichord playing all parts and a bassoon, violone, trombone, or cello on the bass line.

Céleste: Usually an 8' string or flute stop that is tuned either sharp or flat. When used with its "partner" (i.e., a flute or string tuned to A440), the effect is one of a shimmering, undulating tremolo, much like a string player's vibrato.

Choir division: Like the Swell division, the Choir is considered a "secondary" manual, subservient to the Great, providing additional color and reinforcement. It is often enclosed like the Swell division (i.e., pipes are located in a box with shades that open and close, thereby creating variable dynamics).

Chord root: The note upon which a chord is built (e.g., in a G-B-D triad, G is the chord root).

Compound stop: A stop that controls more than one rank or set of pipes; the number of ranks is indicated by the Roman numeral on the stop.

Contemporary period: The period in music history dating approximately from the beginning of the twentieth century to the present day. However, many composers throughout this century have chosen to write in neo-Baroque or neo-Romantic idioms. Some characteristics of contemporary music include the free use of dissonance, the development of new playing techniques, complex rhythmic structures, and nontraditional approaches to organ registration.

Cornet (pronounced kor-náy): A solo color consisting of Flutes 8', 4', 2 ⅔, 2, 1 ⅗. It may also be constructed by adding the Sesquialtera II to the Flutes 8', 4', and 2'. Finally, "cornet," which contains all or part of the ranks listed above may be found as a compound stop.

Coupler: A device that unites one division with another (intermanual couplers) or doubles a manual's existing sound at the octave above or below (intramanual couplers). For example, Swell to Great 8' is an intermanual coupler that causes the stops that are drawn on the Swell to sound at pitch on the Great. Great to Great 4' is an intramanual coupler that causes the stops drawn on the Great to sound at their normal octave and one octave higher.

Crescendo pedal: A device that gradually adds all the stops of the organ.

Détaché (also detached, ordinary, or articulated style): A term describing the basic approach to keyboard touch in music of the sixteenth through eighteenth centuries. Varying degrees of non-legato are possible, from a bright staccato to almost imperceptible non-legato. Choice of articulative patterns should take into account tempo, rhythmic patterns, melodic shape, and natural accents related to strong and weak beats.

Dominant: The pitch that is the fifth of a scale. The pull of the harmonic of the triad built above the dominant is toward tonic. It is identified by the Roman numeral V.

En chamade: A rank of pipes (usually trumpets) placed horizontally in the front of the organ case.

Ensemble: A term suggesting full registrations that produce a sense of blending or homogeneity rather than piquant contrasts.

Expression pedal (also "swell" pedal): The pedal that controls the opening and closing of shades for "enclosed" divisions such as the Swell and Choir.

Flue ranks: Pipes in which sound is made by air traveling through a windway (called a "flue") and interacting with the pipe mouth, much like a flute produces sound. Families of organ tone produced by flue pipes are the principals, flutes, and strings.

Flutes: One of the four families of organ tone. Flute stops can be used as solo colors, either singly or in combination, and can often be used with other families of organ stops due to their high blending potential.

Foundations: Most commonly the flutes and principals at unison and octave sounding pitches (32', 16', 8', 4', 2', 1').

Full organ: Either a registration indication in the score corresponding to *fortissimo* or a separate stop on the organ marked *tutti* or *sforzando,* which immediately adds all, or most, of the organ's stops.

Graded pistons: Starting with softest foundations 8', each piston is set progressively louder until the full ensemble is achieved. Many variations are possible. This general concept may be applied to hymn registration, accompanying, and much repertoire.

Great division: The principal manual division. Except for a few late Romantic experiments, the Great has always been "unenclosed" (i.e., the pipes of this division are not in an enclosed box which has shades), therefore the dynamic of each individual Great rank is invariable.

Hymn intonations: Hymn introductions that may also be used as interludes or bridges between stanzas.

Manual: A keyboard for the hands.

Mixture: A compound stop that is usually comprised of octave- and fifth-sounding principal ranks. For example, a Mixture III commonly denotes a stop that activates three rows of principal pipes sounding the key's actual pitch and a pitch a fifth above. Mixtures are used with the principal chorus (16', 8', 4', 2').

Mutations (or overtone stops): Identified by a fraction, these stops do not play the actual notated pitch but an overtone. The most common are the 2⅔' (or 1⅓'), which is a fifth-sounding rank and the 1⅗' (or 3⅕'), which is a third-sounding rank. For example, middle C on a 2⅔' stop plays the G one octave and a fifth above: middle C on a 1⅗' stop plays the E two octaves and a third above. Mutations are usually used with an 8' fundamental pitch and other stops as desired (see Cornet and Sesquialtera).

Pedal division: The division of pipes controlled by the organ's pedals. Like the Great and Positiv, the Pedal division is most often unenclosed.

Pedal point: A sustained note, usually in the pedal, over or around which changing harmonies occur; useful in hymn variations.

Piston: Buttons that control the stop changes for the manuals and pedal. Divisional pistons affect one manual or the pedal only; general pistons affect the entire organ. All or part may be graded (see above).

Plenum (or Organo Pleno): Principals (16'), 8', 4', 2', and Mixture, with optional reeds.

Positiv division (also "Rückpositif" or "Positif"): Like the Great and Pedal divisions, this secondary manual division is unenclosed. In its purest form, the pipes are located in a separate case behind the organist's back on the gallery railing. The Dutch word for "back" is *rück,* therefore "Rückpositif" literally means the division that is at the organist's back. Some large organs now incorporate both the neo-Baroque Positiv, which is most appropriate for musical effects common in seventeenth- and eighteenth-century music, and enclosed manual divisions such as the Choir and Swell, which are useful for nineteenth- and twentieth-century repertoire.

Principals: One of the four families of organ tone. The principal provides the organ's foundation tone and is the only type of organ tone that does not, in some manner, imitate another instrumental color.

Rank: A set of pipes controlled by an organ stop. Compound stops (see above) control multiple ranks of pipes with one stop or tab.

Reeds: One of the four families of organ tone. Reed stops imitate a wide range of orchestral reed and brass colors. Unlike the flue pipes (principals, flutes, and strings), all reed sound is produced by the vibration of a metal tongue (the "reed"), which is attached to the pipe. (In the case of reed pipes, it is referred to as a "resonator.")

Romantic period: The period in music history dating from the early nineteenth century to the early twentieth century. Romanticism as a musical style, however, can be attributed to many twentieth-century composers (e.g., many works by Louis Vierne). Characteristics may include an emphasis on melody and a general sense of lyricism, highly emotional content, subjectivity in performance, and a predilection for the organ's rich, broad, tonal capabilities and/or orchestral effects.

Sesquialtera: A compound flute stop containing both the 2 ⅔' and 1 ⅗' ranks drawn with the Flute 8' and possibly 4' and 2' (see Cornet above).

Setter button or setter board: Mechanism that sets the pistons. This may take the form of a setter button that is held in while the piston is pushed to set the stops drawn (the so-called "capture" system) or a setter board on which tabs representing stops are moved to the "on" or "off" positions. A third method of setting stops involves holding in the piston while the stop tabs themselves are drawn or canceled.

Shades (also "Swell" shades): The moveable shutters, which, when opened or closed by the expression pedal, control the *crescendi* and *diminuendi* of the Swell or Choir divisions.

Stop: A draw knob or tab that controls one or more ranks of pipes.

Strings: One of the four families of organ tone. String stops imitate a wide range of orchestral colors and may be used singly or in combination with principals and flutes.

Strong beats: The beats that receive the greatest accent or inflection within the measure.

Subdominant: The pitch that is the fourth of a scale. A triad built above this note often leads to the dominant triad (hence the name, *sub*-dominant). The "Amen" cadence, however, is an important example of the subdominant triad resolving to the tonic triad. It is identified by the Roman numeral IV (major key) or iv (minor key).

Swell division: The manual division that is situated in an enclosed box with shades that open and close, thereby creating variable dynamics. It is a secondary manual in relation to the Great manual and provides color, solo capabilities, and reinforcement to the organ's ensemble.

Tonic: The pitch that is the first, and most important, note of a scale. It is identified by the Roman numeral I (major key) or i (minor key).

Tremulant or tremolo: The stop that produces a "vibrato" effect in the sound of all stops drawn.

Unison off: A device that eliminates all sounds drawn at unison pitch on any given division. It does not affect the divisions coupled to this division or intramanual couplers. For example, the Great Unison Off would eliminate all Great stops from sounding, but if the Swell is coupled to Great, all Swell stops still sound, and if the Great to Great 4' is drawn, all Great stops sound one octave higher.

Voice: 1. Another word for rank. 2. The term for the process organ builders follow to develop each pipe's desired timbre, speech, volume, and quality.

Appendix II
Selected Repertoire for Manuals Alone or Manuals with Easy Pedal

The following list provides a basic framework for repertoire selections that address music of a wide historical and stylistic range. You may first wish to purchase repertoire on hymn tunes, wedding and memorial service collections, and one of the basic technique books. Other music may then be added to supplement your "core" service music collection. For your own enjoyment and musical growth, explore a variety of styles and periods—from Bach and Pachelbel to Franck and Vierne.

Alain, Albert	*5 Pieces Faciles,* Philippo & Combre 32861
Bach, J. S.	Individually Transmitted Chorales ("Misc. Chorales" NBA edition vol. 3, Barenreiter)
	Also two- and three-part Inventions and Preludes and Fugues from *The Well-Tempered Clavier*
(Krebs, J. L.)	*8 "Little" Preludes and Fugues,* Kalmus, vol. 8
Beck, Theodore	*5 Hymn Preludes,* Concordia 97-5391
	14 Organ Chorale Preludes, Augsburg 11-6156
Beechey, Gwilym	*5 Preludes on English Hymns,* Concordia 97-5964

Benoit, Dom P.	*Noël Basque,* Belwin Mills FES 7961
Boëllmann, Leon	*Heures Mystiques,* vols. 1 and 2, Kalmus
Burkhardt, Michael	*5 Lenten Hymn Improvisations,* Morning Star 10-309
	5 Easter Hymn Improvisations, Morning Star 10-403
	Music for Manuals (Advent and Christmas), Morning Star 10-001, 10-010
Callahan, Charles	*6 Meditations on English Hymns,* Concordia 97-6189
	5 Improvisations on Communion Hymns, Concordia 97-6126
Couperin, François	*Mass for the Convents,* Kalmus 3315
Drischner, Max	*Choralevorspiele,* Schultheiss CLS 202
Eggert, John	*6 Hymn Preludes,* Concordia, set 1, 97-5893, set 2, 97-5912
Ferko, Frank	*Hymn Preludes,* Augsburg 11-6800
Franck, César	*L'Organiste (59 Pieces),* Kalmus KO 5433
Gibbs, Allen Orton	*Music for Sunday Morning,* Concordia (#14 in series)
Held, Wilbur	*Preludes and Postludes* (vol. 1), Augsburg 11-9318
	7 Settings of American Folk Hymns, Concordia 97-5829
	A Nativity Suite, Concordia 97-4461
	A Suite of Passion Hymns, Concordia 97-4843
	6 Preludes on Easter Hymns, Concordia 97-5330
	Hymn Preludes for Pentecost, Concordia 97-5517
Hopson, Hal	*Praise to the Lord,* SMP KK389
Johnson, David N.	*Manuals Only,* Augsburg 11-9290
	Music for Worship, Augsburg 11-9297
	Wondrous Love, Augsburg 11-0821
Lang, C. S.	*20 Hymn-Tune Preludes,* Oxford
Langlais, Jean	*Organ Book (10 Pieces),* Elkan-Vogel 463-0006
Manz, Paul	*10 Chorale Improvisations,* Concordia 97-4554, 97-4656
Martin, Gilbert	*2 Meditations for Christmas,* H. W. Gray 943
Mendelssohn, Felix	*Prelude in G Major and Selected Movements from Sonatas,* Novello 01 0215 or complete in Kalmus edition
Micheelsen, H. F.	*The Holstein Little Organ Book,* Barenreiter 1679
	Organisten Praxis (4 vols.), Hullenhagen and Griehl
Monnikendam, Marius	*12 Inventions,* World Library of Sacred Music 0-5532
Nelhybel, Vaclav	*3 danses liturgigues,* G. Schirmer 394
Owens, Sam Batt	*5 Little Romantic Preludes,* Augsburg 11-6033
Pachelbel, Johann	*Selected Organ Works,* Barenreiter
Peeters, Flor	*Hymn Preludes for the Liturgical Year* (in 24 vols.) major celebrations vols. 1, 2, 3, Peters ed. Aria, Heuwekemeijer 265
Vierne, Louis	*24 Pieces en style libre* (2 vols.), complete in Masters ed.
Willan, Healey	*36 Short Preludes and Postludes* (3 vols.), Peters
Wood, Dale	*Brother James's Air,* S.M.P. 58
	Preludes and Postludes (vol. 3), Augsburg
Wyton, Alec	*Nativity Suite,* Flammer HF-5019

Collections

Advent and Christmas Book (2 vols.), Lorenz ACOP C2, KK 457C2
An Easy Album, Oxford O 19 375125 9
Concordia Hymn Prelude Series (42 vols.) vols. 1-6 Advent/Christmas/Epiphany; vols.
    7-9 Lent; vols. 10-11 Easter; Concordia Publ.
80 Chorale Preludes (ed. Keller), Peters 11354
For Manuals Only, Oxford 0 19 375131 3
Hymntune Preludes (2 vols.), Augsburg
Hymn Preludes for Holy Communion in 3 vols., Concordia
Old English Organ Music for Manuals (ed. Trevor), in 6 vols., Oxford
One Hundred Hymn Preludes, Kevin Mayhew 0 86209 441 0
Organ Chorales of the 17th and 18th Centuries, Kalmus 4482
Organ Music for Funerals and Memorial Services, Augsburg 11-6725, 11-7626
The Organist's Library: A Collection for Manuals in 4 vols., Mayhew
Seasonal Chorale Preludes for Manuals (ed. Trevor), in 2 vols., Oxford
Wedding Music in 2 vols., Concordia
Wedding Album for Manuals (ed. Trevor), Oxford
Wedding Music in 5 vols., (ed. Johnson), Augsburg

Hymnals

The following hymnals or tune collections have simplified accompaniments.

Cooper, Janette	*Hymn Tunes for the Reluctant Organist,* Oxford
Leupold, Wayne	*Easiest Hymns,* Wayne Leupold Editions
The Hymnal 1982 (Episcopal):	Simplified Accompaniment edition (Contains 96 hymns and selected service music), Church Hymnal Corporation
The Baptist Hymnal (1991):	Simplified Piano Edition (contains 200 hymns), Genevox Music

Technique Books

Davis, Roger	*The Organists' Manual,* W. W. Norton
Enright, Richard	*Fundamentals of Organ Playing,* Concordia
Leupold, Wayne	*First Organ Book,* Wayne Leupold Editions, Inc., ECS Publishing, Boston
Gleason, Harold	*Method of Organ Playing,* 8th ed., Prentice-Hall
Ritchie, George and George Stauffer	*Organ Technique: Modern and Early,* Prentice-Hall

Appendix III
Other Resources

Shoes

Organmaster Shoes (men and women)
282 Stepstone Hill
Guilford, CT 06437

Capezio Tap Shoes Style No. 400 "Tyette" (women's)
or Capezio character shoes (for men)

Organizations

National: The American Guild of Organists (AGO)
475 Riverside Drive, Suite 1260
New York, NY 10115

Denominational:

American Baptist Association:	The National Fellowship of Music Leaders 501-455-4588
American Baptist Churches USA:	The Fellowship of American Baptist Musicians 313-277-7995
Disciples of Christ:	Association of Disciple Musicians 317-635-3100
Church of the Brethren:	Association of the Arts 708-742-5100
Episcopal:	Anglican Association of Musicians 501-372-2512
Jewish Organizations:	Guild of Temple Musicians 301-833-2467
Lutheran Church:	The Association of Lutheran Musicians 1-800-624-2526
Presbyterian Church USA:	Presbyterian Association of Musicians 502-569-5000
Roman Catholic:	National Association of Pastoral Musicians 202-723-5800
Southern Baptist:	Southern Baptist Church Music Conference 615-251-2944

Unitarian Universalist Assoc.:   Unitarian Universalist Musicians
                                                   Network
                                                   617-742-2100
United Methodist: Fellowship of United Methodists
                                                   in Music and Other Worship
                                                   Arts
                                                   615-340-7453

(More information regarding denominational support for church musicians can be found in *Church Musicians' Guide to the Denominations in Canada and the United States,* Second Edition, 1994, published by and available from the American Guild of Organists.)

Useful Texts

Arnold, Corliss Richard. *Organ Literature, A Comprehensive Survey.* Third edition. Metuchen, N.J.: Scarecrow Press, 1995.

Booty, John E. *The Church in History.* San Francisco: Harper SanFrancisco, 1979.

Bower, Peter ed. *A Guide for the Common Lectionary.* Philadelphia: Geneva Press, 1987.

Hamill, Paul (publisher). *Church Music Handbook.* Gemini Press. Published annually (distributed by Theodore Presser).

Hatchett, Marion. *A Guide to the Practice of Church Music.* New York: Church Hymnal Corporation, 1989.

Hickman, Hoyt, Don Saliers, Laurence Stookey, and James F. White. *Handbook of the Christian Year.* Nashville: Abingdon Press, 1986.

Hurford, Peter. *Making Music on the Organ.* Oxford: Oxford University Press, 1988.

Schmidt, Dennis. *Hymnal Studies Seven: An Organist's Guide to Resources for the Hymnal 1982.* New York: Church Hymnal Corporation, 1987.

Soderlund, Sandra. *A Guide to the Pipe Organ.* Wayne Leupold Editions, 1995.

Walton, Janet. *Art and Worship: A Vital Connection.* Collegeville: The Liturgical Press, 1988.

Westermeyer, Paul. *The Church Musician.* New York: Harper & Row, 1988.

Williams, Peter and Barbara Owen. *The Organ.* (From The New Grove Musical Instrument Series) New York: W. W. Norton, 1980.

There are also many useful educational resources published by the AGO and by denominational organizations. See *The American Organist* magazine and your denomination's music publications for these resources.